ENSEMBLE DEVELOPMENT
Chorales and Warm-up Exercises for Tone, Technique and Rhythm
YOUNG CONCERT BAND

Peter **BOONSHAFT** | Chris **BERNOTAS**

Thank you for making *Sound Innovations Ensemble Development for Young Concert Band* a part of your large ensemble curriculum. With 167 exercises, including more than 100 chorales by some of today's most renowned young band composers, this book will be a valuable resource in helping you grow in your understanding and abilities as an ensemble musician.

An assortment of exercises, grouped by key, are presented in a variety of young band difficulty levels. Where possible, several exercises in the same category are provided to allow variety while accomplishing the goals of that specific type of exercise. You will notice that many exercises and chorales are clearly marked with dynamics, articulations, style and tempo for you to practice those aspects of performance. Other exercises are intentionally left for you or your teacher to determine how best to use them in reaching your performance goals.

Whether you are progressing through exercises to better your technical facility or challenging your musicianship with beautiful chorales, we are confident you will be excited, motivated and inspired by using *Sound Innovations Ensemble Development for Young Concert Band.*

ISBN-10: 1-4706-3388-4
ISBN-13: 978-1-4706-3388-2

Instrument photos courtesy of Yamaha Corporation of America Band & Orchestral Division

2

Concert B♭ Major (Your C Major)

1 LONG TONES

2 PASSING THE TONIC

3 PASSING THE TONIC

4 PITCH MATCHING: WOODWIND MOUTHPIECES WITH BAND ACCOMPANIMENT

† *Match the pitch on the mouthpiece and barrel/neck.*

5 SCALE BUILDER

6 SCALE BUILDER

3

7   EXPANDING INTERVALS: DIATONIC

8   EXPANDING INTERVALS: CHROMATIC

9   INTERVAL BUILDER: DIATONIC INTERVALS

10   INTERVAL BUILDER: PERFECT INTERVALS

11   CHORD BUILDER

12   CHORD BUILDER

13   MOVING CHORD TONES

14 DIATONIC HARMONY

15 DIATONIC HARMONY

16 RHYTHMIC SOUNDS

Play the repeated section at least 4 times.

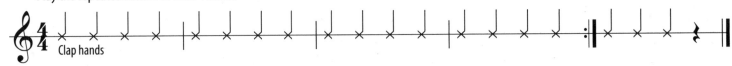

Clap hands

17 RHYTHMIC SUBDIVISION

18 5-NOTE SCALE

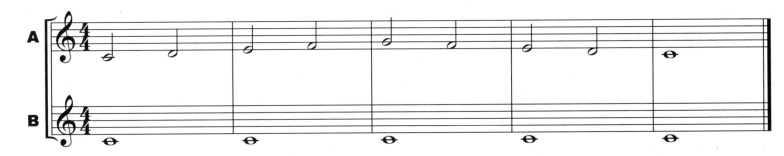

19 CANON: 5-NOTE SCALE

20 CANON: 6-NOTE SCALE

21 CANON: 8-NOTE SCALE

22 CHORALE: 5-NOTE SCALE

Chris M. Bernotas (ASCAP)

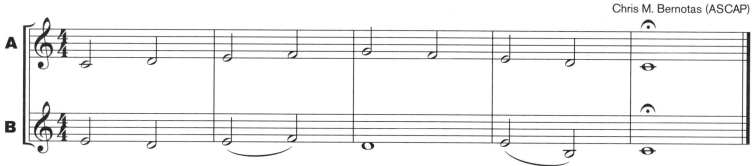

23 CHORALE: 5-NOTE SCALE

Chris M. Bernotas (ASCAP)

24 CHORALE: 6-NOTE SCALE

Chris M. Bernotas (ASCAP)

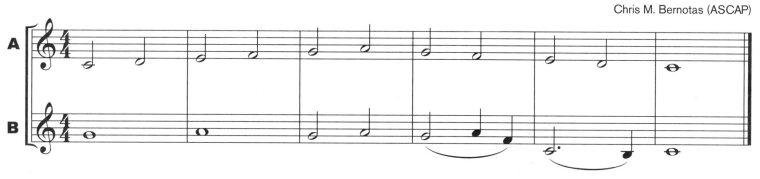

25 CHORALE: 8-NOTE SCALE

Chris M. Bernotas (ASCAP)

26 CHORALE: 8-NOTE SCALE

Chris M. Bernotas (ASCAP)

6

27 **CHORALE**

Robert Sheldon (ASCAP)

28 **CHORALE**

Moderato

John O'Reilly (ASCAP)

29 **CHORALE**

Ralph Ford (ASCAP)

30 **CHORALE**

Moderately

Michael Story (ASCAP)

31 **CHORALE**

Randall D. Standridge (ASCAP)

32 **CHORALE**

Roland Barrett (ASCAP)

33 **CHORALE**

Slowly

Chris M. Bernotas (ASCAP)

34 **CHORALE**

Rob Grice (ASCAP)

8

43 **CHORALE**

Ralph Ford (ASCAP)

44 **CHORALE**

John O'Reilly (ASCAP)

Andante

45 **CHORALE**

"Finally the first smells of Summer were in the air. 'Time to plant those strange seeds we found,' she thought."

Jodie Blackshaw (ASCAP)

46 **CHORALE**

Matt Conaway (ASCAP)

Gently flowing

47 **CHORALE**

Randall D. Standridge (ASCAP)

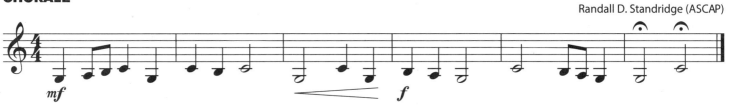

48 **CHORALE**

Robert Sheldon (ASCAP)

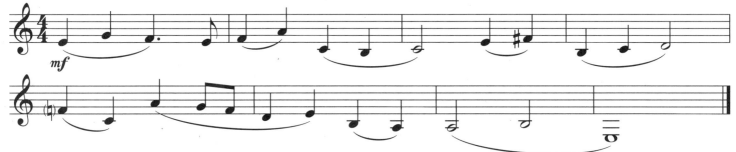

49 **CHORALE**

Chris M. Bernotas (ASCAP)

Slowly

50 **CHORALE**

Roland Barrett (ASCAP)

Concert G Minor (Your A Minor)

51 LONG TONES

52 PASSING THE TONIC

53 EXPANDING INTERVALS: DIATONIC

54 INTERVAL BUILDER: DIATONIC INTERVALS

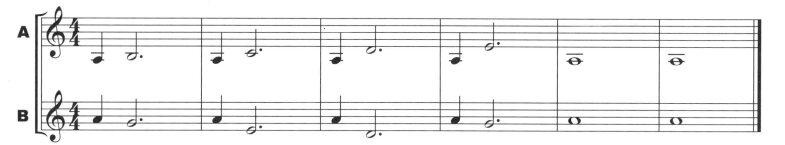

55 CHORD BUILDER

56 DIATONIC HARMONY

57 CHORALE: 5-NOTE SCALE

Chris M. Bernotas (ASCAP)

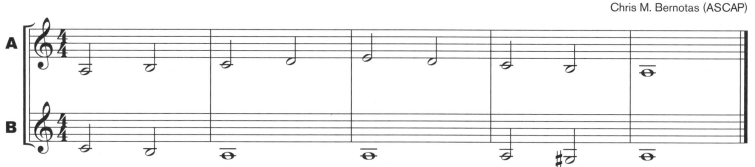

58 **CHORALE: 8-NOTE SCALE (NATURAL MINOR)**

Chris M. Bernotas (ASCAP)

59 **CHORALE: 8-NOTE SCALE (HARMONIC MINOR)**

Chris M. Bernotas (ASCAP)

60 **CHORALE**

Tyler S. Grant (ASCAP)

61 **CHORALE**

Rob Grice (ASCAP)

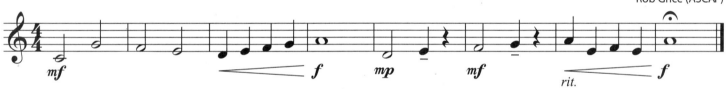

62 **CHORALE**

Robert Sheldon (ASCAP)

63 **CHORALE**

Michael Story (ASCAP)

64 **CHORALE**

Randall D. Standridge (ASCAP)

11

12

Concert E♭ Major (Your F Major)

73 **LONG TONES**

74 **LONG TONES**

75 **PASSING THE TONIC**

76 **PASSING THE TONIC**

77 **SCALE BUILDER**

78 **SCALE BUILDER**

79 EXPANDING INTERVALS: DIATONIC

80 EXPANDING INTERVALS: CHROMATIC

81 INTERVAL BUILDER: DIATONIC INTERVALS

82 INTERVAL BUILDER: PERFECT INTERVALS

83 CHORD BUILDER

84 CHORD BUILDER

85 MOVING CHORD TONES

14

86 DIATONIC HARMONY

87 DIATONIC HARMONY

88 RHYTHMIC SUBDIVISION

89 5-NOTE SCALE

90 CANON: 5-NOTE SCALE

91 CANON: 6-NOTE SCALE

92 CANON: 8-NOTE SCALE

15

93 **CHORALE: 5-NOTE SCALE**

Chris M. Bernotas (ASCAP)

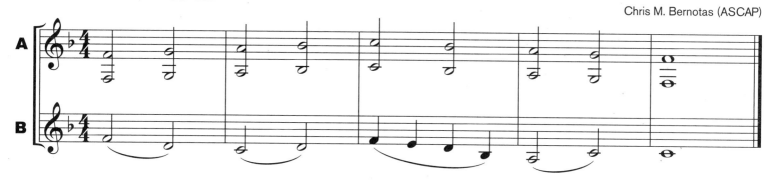

94 **CHORALE: 5-NOTE SCALE**

Chris M. Bernotas (ASCAP)

95 **CHORALE: 6-NOTE SCALE**

Chris M. Bernotas (ASCAP)

96 **CHORALE: 8-NOTE SCALE**

Chris M. Bernotas (ASCAP)

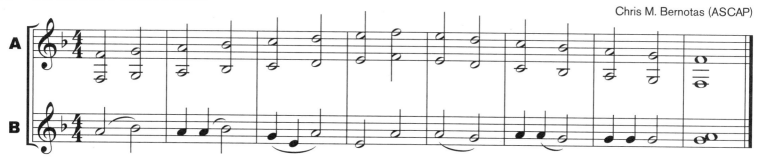

97 **CHORALE: 8-NOTE SCALE**

Chris M. Bernotas (ASCAP)

98 CHORALE

Todd Stalter (ASCAP)

Maestoso

99 CHORALE

Michael Story (ASCAP)

Moderately slow

100 CHORALE

Rob Grice (ASCAP)

Gently

101 CHORALE

Matt Conaway (ASCAP)

Gently

102 CHORALE

John O'Reilly (ASCAP)

Moderato

103 CHORALE

Scott Watson (BMI)

Moderato

rit.

104 CHORALE

Roland Barrett (ASCAP)

105 CHORALE

Ralph Ford (ASCAP)

Espressivo

rit.

17

114 **CHORALE**

John O'Reilly (ASCAP)

Andante

115 **CHORALE**

Michael Story (ASCAP)

Moderately slow

116 **CHORALE**

Todd Stalter (ASCAP)

Andante

117 **CHORALE**

Randall D. Standridge (ASCAP)

118 **CHORALE**

Scottish Psalter, 1635
Arranged by Scott Watson (BMI)

Maestoso

1

2

119 **CHORALE**

Jodie Blackshaw (ASCAP)

"Heart pounding he opened his eyes. A dull light grew to reveal a world he had never seen before."

120 **CHORALE**

Chris M. Bernotas (ASCAP)

Slowly

121 **CHORALE**

Matt Conaway (ASCAP)

Concert C Minor (Your D Minor)

22 LONG TONES

23 PASSING THE TONIC

24 EXPANDING INTERVALS: DIATONIC

25 INTERVAL BUILDER: DIATONIC INTERVALS

26 CHORD BUILDER

27 DIATONIC HARMONY

28 CHORALE: 5-NOTE SCALE

Chris M. Bernotas (ASCAP)

129 **CHORALE: 8-NOTE SCALE (NATURAL MINOR)**

Chris M. Bernotas (ASCAP)

130 **CHORALE: 8-NOTE SCALE (HARMONIC MINOR)**

Chris M. Bernotas (ASCAP)

131 **CHORALE**

Tyler S. Grant (ASCAP)

Slowly

132 **CHORALE**

Rob Grice (ASCAP)

133 **CHORALE**

Ralph Ford (ASCAP)

134 **CHORALE**

Robert Sheldon (ASCAP)

135 **CHORALE**

Michael Story (ASCAP)

Moderately slow

22

Concert F Major (Your G Major)

144 PASSING THE TONIC

145 EXPANDING INTERVALS: CHROMATIC

146 CHORD BUILDER

147 DIATONIC HARMONY

148 CHORALE: 6-NOTE SCALE

Chris M. Bernotas (ASCAP)

149 CHORALE

Rob Grice (ASCAP)

150 CHORALE

Ralph Ford (ASCAP)

151 CHORALE

Scott Watson (BMI)

152 CHORALE

Randall D. Standridge (ASCAP)

153 CHORALE

John O'Reilly (ASCAP)

154 CHORALE

Roland Barrett (ASCAP)

155 CHORALE

Adapted from Psalm 150, Claude Goudimel
Arranged by Todd Stalter (ASCAP)

Concert D Minor (Your E Minor)

156 PASSING THE TONIC

157 CHORD BUILDER

158 DIATONIC HARMONY

159 CHORALE: 8-NOTE SCALE (HARMONIC MINOR)

Chris M. Bernotas (ASCAP)

160 CHORALE

Roland Barrett (ASCAP)

161 CHORALE

Robert Sheldon (ASCAP)

162 CHORALE

Todd Stalter (ASCAP)

163 CHORALE

Scott Watson (BMI)

164 CHORALE

Michael Story (ASCAP)

165 CHORALE

Ralph Ford (ASCAP)

166 CHORALE

Tyler S. Grant (ASCAP)

167 CHORALE

Jodie Blackshaw (ASCAP)

"In the darkness all she could hear was the sound of her beating heart. What had she done?"